I Feel...
SOMETHING

Words and pictures by

DJ Corchin

sourcebooks
eXplore

Sometimes I feel **something**.
It's hard to explain.

It's not quite a **feeling**.
It's not quite a pain.

The **inside** of my body

is like a **runaway** train.

The things that I'm **feeling** make no sense in my **brain**.

Sometimes I feel **furious** when I thought I was fine.

My **heart** was just racing,

but I **missed** all the signs.

Suddenly I'm **screaming,**

and I'm no longer **kind**.

Then I realize I'm just **hot** in this sweater of mine.

I'm surprisingly anxious and might start to **cry**...

when really I'm **hungry**

for this **big** piece of pie.

Boom!

Snap!

CRACK!

Bam!

I'm thinking I'm **scared**
of the noises close by,

but it's just my own heart going
THUMP-THUMP inside.

I could try **meditation**
and scan all my parts.

I could draw all my **muscles** and make some muscly art.

I could take a few guesses
of the speed of my **heart**,

then write them all down
on a **glittery** chart.

62	124	72	84
133	65	121	91
67	71	73	115
72	64	127	75

There are things that I **sense**
that are inside of me.

I could be **hungry** or **sick,**

or just have to **pee**.

Although sometimes I **feel** like I don't have a guide.

I'm learning to share when
I **feel** something inside.

I Feel...
SOMETHING

What is this feeling inside my body?

If my tummy is growling, I might need lunch. If my arm is tingly and uncomfortable, I might have an itch. We all have sensations within our bodies that tell us things like we're hungry, hot or cold, or feeling sick. **Interoception** is the ability to understand what those sensations in our bodies mean. Some people struggle with identifying and understanding those sensations. That can affect all kinds of things such as their ability to communicate how they're feeling because they can't recognize or explain the sensations in their body.

This book is a simple introduction to the concept of interoception. If you'd like to learn more or if you have questions, there are doctors and therapists who specialize in helping people learn to listen to and understand their bodies. You can start by talking with your family doctor. For now, here are some activities to get to know your body better!

Body Drawing

By understanding all the parts in your body,
you can understand the sensations you feel inside.

1. Draw an outline of your body with a head, neck, arms, hands, torso, legs, and feet.

2. Draw the parts that are located inside any body area you wish, or maybe in the area where you're feeling something.
   You can ask an adult for help in discovering what the muscles in your leg look like, or the organs inside your torso, for example.

3. You can draw multiple copies of the body outline, one for muscles, organs, bones, etc.

4. You can keep the drawings to help identify where these sensations are and what the sensations you feel might be.

Heart Chart

1. Find a watch or heart monitor that will allow you to track your heart rate.

2. On a poster board or piece of paper, write down five physical activities you like to do.

3. Each one should have a different degree of difficulty, like running, bowling, dancing, or push-ups.

4. Write down what your heart rate is for each activity using the heart monitor.

5. Which activities have higher heart rates? Why do you think that happens?

6. You can continue to add to the list as you think of more activities!

Sensation Fixation Documentation Creation

In other words, let's make a journal for how your body might feel inside during certain activities!

1. You can use a premade sketchbook for this activity, or make your own by folding together pieces of paper and stapling them in the middle.

2. Each time you experience a new sensation, write a journal entry for what you were doing and what you felt inside.

3. You can draw an I Feel... face of how you felt, or describe what happened afterwards, or both!

4. When you're not sure if you've felt a sensation before, you can review your journal entries to help you remember.

Sensation Words

Having the words to describe a sensation is just as important as understanding what the sensation means. Here is a fun activity to help build your sensation vocabulary.

1. With a friend or trusted adult, make a list of as many sensation words as you can think of. Words like tickled, hot, scratchy, squished, sharp, or gassy are all good examples.

2. Using different colors of construction paper, draw and cut out fun word bubbles for as many words as you have. You can make them all different shapes and sizes.

3. You can use your body chart from the previous activity, or draw an outline of a new body on a new piece of paper.

4. Whenever you feel a sensation, you can use the word bubbles to describe where and how you're feeling by putting them next to the corresponding area on the body outline.

5. You can use multiple words to describe a sensation, such as both sweaty and scratchy.

6. Continue to build your word library and add more bubbles as you talk about them with your friends or caring adult.

It is ALWAYS OK to ask someone for help when you are feeling bad.

The I Feel... Children's Series is a resource created to assist in discussions about emotional awareness.

The activities listed here are simple, fun suggestions; however, please contact a professional in who specializes with interoception for activities specific to an individual's needs.

To James

Copyright © 2018, 2021 by The phazelFOZ Company, LLC
Cover and internal design © 2021 by Sourcebooks

Sourcebooks and the colophon are registered trademarks of Sourcebooks.

All rights reserved.

The characters and events portrayed in this book are fictitious or are used fictitiously.
Any similarity to real persons, living or dead, is purely coincidental and not intended by the author.

Published by Sourcebooks eXplore, an imprint of Sourcebooks Kids
P.O. Box 4410, Naperville, Illinois 60567-4410
(630) 961-3900
sourcebookskids.com

Originally published in 2018 in the United States of America by The phazelFOZ Company, LLC.

Library of Congress Cataloging-in-Publication Data is on file with the publisher.

Source of Production: 1010 Printing Asia Limited, North Point, Hong Kong, China
Date of Production: November 2020
Run Number: 5019657

Printed and bound in China.
OGP 10 9 8 7 6 5 4 3 2 1